# One Horse,
# One Hundred Miles,
# One Day

Written and illustrated by

## Sam Savitt

1   2   3   4   5   6   7   8   9   10


Library of Congress Cataloging in Publication Data

Savitt, Sam.
One horse, one hundred miles, one day.

Includes index.
1. Tevis Cup Ride.   I. Title.
SF296.E5S28        798.4        80-2777
ISBN  0-396-07935-0        AACR1

## ACKNOWLEDGMENTS

I am grateful to Went Tellington, Wendell Robie, and Charles Barieau for their valuable cooperation, and I wish especially to thank Kathy Tellington and Dr. Richard Barsaleau for actively participating in this book.

*To my good friend Went Tellington,*
*without whom this book would never have come about*

# one

I have been involved in the equestrian world for over thirty years. I have sketched, painted, and written about fox hunting, flat racing, steeplechasing, eventing, dressage, grand prix jumping, polo, and rodeo.

Several years ago, I first became aware of endurance riding, but I gave it little attention. I thought—what was so difficult about riding a horse from one point to the next? What a bore that could be. As with things we know little about, I was inclined to underestimate what went into it.

After a bit of prodding from Wentworth Tellington, governor of the Western States Trail Foundation, I decided to find out more about endurance riding. I learned that the purpose is to approach the limits of stress for horse and rider to the point where there is no problem in differentiating between horses for purpose of selection. I also learned that these rides include contests of twenty-five miles or over in one day, to a hundred miles or more. I then got to thinking specifically about the

annual Western States 100 Miles One Day Endurance Race, usually referred to as the Tevis Cup Ride—the most demanding endurance ride in the world.

Wendell Robie, the president of Heart Federal Savings and Loan Association, is the originator and moving force behind this famous ride. He is a tough, lean, energetic man in his eighties who has ridden the Tevis many times since its inception in 1955.

Robie is a native Californian, and he is referred to often as the "father of modern-day endurance riding." The following little story that he told to me will help the reader gain a better insight into the kind of man he is.

"When I was managing the family lumber business in Benson, Arizona," he related, "I happened to have a three-year-old unshod mare I was just breaking. I was told that a small boy had been injured up on the top of Mount Lemon, some forty-two miles away. There had been a big slide and the road was closed, and I was asked if I could take some medicine up there quickly on horseback.

"I was familiar with the mountain and immediately headed from Tucson to the beginning of the historic soldier's trail which had been used to supply the old Indian defense post at Fort Lowell. I rode all night and reached the top of the mountain before daylight to make my delivery.

"My mare was a bit footsore so, with the help of a ranger, I shod her for the return trip before I started back."

Robie's eyes twinkled. "We covered some eighty-six miles in less than a day and I arrived in my office in time to get some work done in the afternoon."

Then, one day in 1955, Wendell was out riding with a group of friends. Along the way they got to arguing about whether the horses of the Pony Express were better than those of today.

"I figure horses are better now than they were then," Wendell declared. He suggested that they prove it one way or another with a ride of one hundred miles in one day. It was decided that the ride should be over the Western States Trail, which climbs from Squaw Valley to the Emigrant Trail Monument on the trail crest of the Sierra Nevadas. From that point the land spreads out into a panorama of unforgettable beauty. Lake Tahoe lies to the east beneath rugged mountains and snow-capped peaks. To the west, north, and south are timbered slopes, rising and falling into deep canyons as they fade off into the blue distance. The trail ends at the fairgrounds in Auburn, California.

This was the route that had been used by the Wells Fargo Express riders in 1852 when they carried mail and treasure for the many mining camps along the Gold Rush section of this same trail.

Wendell Robie asked the University of California School of Veterinary Medicine to provide veterinarians to check the horses. The skeptical directors of the Humane Society sent eight of its people to check at Robinson Flat, the first rest stop about thirty-five miles out on the trail. They backed up their team with a deputy sheriff and a man from the district attorney's office, ready to arrest anyone who abused his horse.

They did not arrest anyone. Only one rider dropped out, and the horses were in good shape. The SPCA checked once

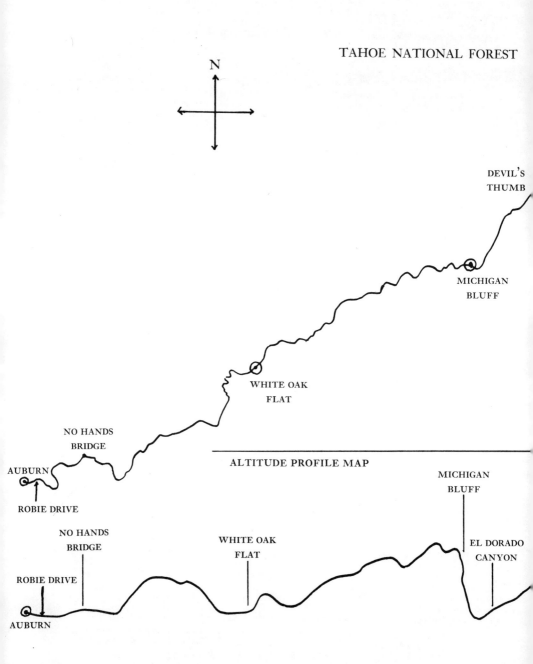

TAHOE NATIONAL FOREST

N

DEVIL'S
THUMB

MICHIGAN
BLUFF

WHITE OAK
FLAT

NO HANDS
BRIDGE

ALTITUDE PROFILE MAP

AUBURN

MICHIGAN
BLUFF

ROBIE DRIVE

NO HANDS
BRIDGE

WHITE OAK
FLAT

EL DORADO
CANYON

ROBIE DRIVE

AUBURN

MAP OF THE WESTERN STATES 100 MILES ONE DAY ENDURANCE RACE OVER

THE CREST OF THE SIERRA NEVADA IN CALIFORNIA—THE TEVIS CUP RIDE

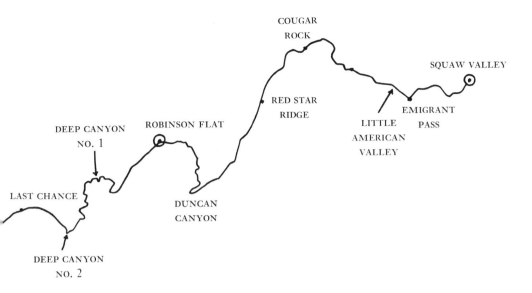

COUGAR
ROCK

SQUAW VALLEY

RED STAR
RIDGE

EMIGRANT
PASS

LITTLE
AMERICAN
VALLEY

DEEP CANYON
NO. 1

ROBINSON FLAT

LAST CHANCE

DUNCAN
CANYON

DEEP CANYON
NO. 2

EL DORADO NATIONAL FOREST

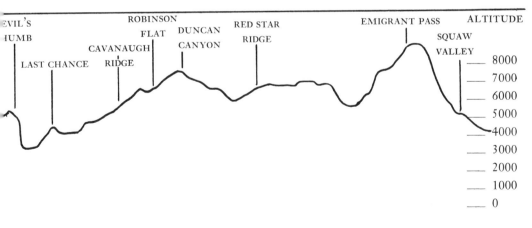

ROBINSON
FLAT

DUNCAN
CANYON

RED STAR
RIDGE

EMIGRANT PASS

ALTITUDE

EVIL'S
HUMB

SQUAW
VALLEY

CAVANAUGH
RIDGE

LAST CHANCE

____ 8000

____ 7000

____ 6000

____ 5000

____ 4000

____ 3000

____ 2000

____ 1000

____ 0

more at Michigan Bluff, about fifty miles into the ride, and the Society has been a strong supporter of the "hundred miler" ever since.

There have been few serious mishaps on this ride. However, what might have been a tragedy happened in 1965 when a horse slipped off the trail above deep El Dorado Canyon. The rider managed to clamber back up to solid ground, but the horse slid downward to a narrow ledge high above the canyon floor.

A cargo helicopter was called in to airlift the trapped animal from this precarious position. But first, a tree growing out of the ledge had to be cut down to allow the helicopter to get in close enough to make the pickup. The Forest Service was unable to bring power equipment to the scene, but a two-man saw finally did the job. Even so, the helicopter's rotor blades whirled so close to the mountainside that bits of brush and sand rained down upon the rescue operation until it was safely completed.

Wendell Robie won the first ride on an Arabian horse named Smoke. No time was kept then. It was not until 1961 that elapsed riding time was recorded.

All agreed this endurance event should be conducted once a year, and that it would be fitting to call it the Tevis Cup Ride, after Lloyd Tevis who had been the director of Wells Fargo from 1872 to 1892.

That's the way the famous Tevis Ride began, but, to me, riding one hundred miles in one day on one horse over that rough country still sounded nearly impossible. So one summer I went out there to see the race for myself. It was then that I

began to perceive what makes an endurance horse—the type, the breed—and the months of dedicated conditioning it takes to prepare a mount for this hundred miler.

With sketch pad and notebook, I followed the ride as best I could, on foot and by vehicle. I had ridden the last ten miles the day before the race to gain a better feel of the land on horseback. When the race was over, I believe I was as exhausted as the people who actually rode in it, and I had developed a tremendous respect for all the horses and riders who had participated.

I had thought I knew the meaning of endurance, but the Tevis Cup Ride gave it a dimension I'd never dreamed of and left me with a question that still haunts me: "I wonder if *I* could do it?"

# two

It is the Friday before the Tevis Cup Ride. The contestants are gathering in Squaw Valley for the pre-race veterinarian check. A good many of them, horses and riders, are veterans of other endurance rides, but this is the big one. It is the most demanding endurance ride in the country, a contest to see who will be among the first ten to finish. But more importantly, it is a challenge to hundreds of ordinary horse people to see if they can do it—just to see if they and the horses they have conditioned for months can complete the one hundred miles over this big country within the 24-hour limit. The rider's motto might be, "To get the farthest, the fastest, in the best condition, and still have enough horse left over to do it again soon."

Where else can an ordinary person participate in an experience that challenges the best and get to know what it feels like to try an Olympic-level event?

Some of these contestants have completed this ride more

than ten times, but again each year comes the challenge: "Can I make it one more time?"

There will be many heartbreaks on this big ride. A contestant who literally has planned for years may find, at the last minute, that his horse comes up lame or injures itself on the trails. Or any one of a dozen other things can happen.

On this day, Squaw Valley Arena is jam-packed with vehicles and horse trailers of every description, bearing license plates from all parts of the United States and Canada. Some contestants have put together metal paddocks where their horses can relax before the vet check.

There are over two hundred entries assembled here. The minimum age limit for riders is twelve. Those riders aged twelve through seventeen must at all times be accompanied by and responsible to the same adult contestant.

The horses must be serviceably sound and at least five years of age. They must never be overridden, left unattended, or in any way abused. They must also carry 165 pounds minimum, as required for international events. At the finish, only the first twenty riders will be weighed in with tack.

The horses I am accustomed to seeing in the East are Thoroughbreds and thoroughbred types—tall, well rounded, and big moving. These horses are something else. There seems to be a variety of breeds present, but for the most part they are Arab or part Arab.

John Summerlin, one of America's top endurance riders, says: "I think it is a foregone conclusion that the Arab is the endurance horse." He feels that other breeds can do well but it takes a lighter breed to be an outstanding horse. He has pointed out that his own horse, Raff Zi, a seven-eighths Arab, 14.2 hands high and 850 pounds, carried his 200-pound weight with no trouble.

Donna Fitzgerald, a five-time winner of the Tevis Ride and holder of five 100-mile buckles, one awarded for each completed ride, pretty much agrees with this. "For the last seven years," says Donna, "I have used only purebred Arabian geldings. I think most other endurance riders also prefer this breed.

An Arabian will take care of himself. When he's tired, he'll slow up and rest. He's a wiry little horse, too, and just seems to have more endurance. Also he's not as apt to give you lameness problems as are other breeds. For instance, a Quarter Horse has big muscles which are apt to tie up."

It is not too difficult to understand why the Arabian horse dominates the field of endurance riding because, if there is one quality that stands above others in the Arabian, it is stamina. His is the oldest and purest breed, because the Arabs of the desert have been interested in keeping it pure for nearly five thousand years.

Three major factors influence a horse's wind. He must have wide-flaring nostrils in order to suck in plenty of air. He must have a big "throttle" and windpipe, and he must have a deep broad chest and barrel to provide plenty of room for his lungs. The Arab breeder bred for these characteristics and got them.

Arabs have proved their substance and bottom by winning first place in a large percentage of the long-distance races held in the United States.

Crabbet, a purebred Arabian gelding, gained fame some time ago by winning a 96-mile race in 1918 and another of a hundred miles that same year. He had his greatest triumph when he won first place in the third of a series of endurance rides for the United States Mounted Service Cup held October 10-14, 1921. This event was an especially grueling contest over 310 miles of macadam and concrete roads. Carrying a weight of 245 pounds, Crabbet finished a full twenty minutes ahead of the rest of the field, with a total traveling time of forty-nine hours four minutes for the five consecutive days of the race.

Of the seventeen horses entered, only seven were able to finish
and, when the tests for condition were conducted the following morning, the indomitable Crabbet was adjudged to be in
nearly perfect condition, and he was one of the few horses
able to gallop freely with no signs of lameness acquired from
the ordeal.

Those who have studied the Arab horse in his native habitat are not astonished at such records of stamina. Horses of the Bedouins have always been esteemed for their ability to travel great distances rapidly without suffering fatigue. That is the standard for which they have been bred through the centuries. It is not uncommon for the horses of the desert to travel across the burning sands without food or water for forty-eight hours at a stretch.

There is a record dated July 27, 1840, which credits an Arab with traveling four hundred miles in four consecutive days.

Another breed Donna Fitzgerald feels could do well in endurance is the Thoroughbred—but he must carry a knowledgeable rider who can rate him, she adds, because a Thoroughbred will run until he's completely out of gas, whereas an Arab will pace himself.

To sum the whole thing up, an endurance horse should have good legs, and be sound and healthy. Size isn't important, good conformation is—a long neck, to allow freedom of shoulders and front legs, and a short back, which carries weight better than does a long back.

All day Friday, riders lead their mounts to the sign-in area where they receive a number to carry throughout the ride. Then they move into an enormous fenced-in field where teams of vets examine the horses, checking pulse rate and respiration. I hear one of the vets, Dr. Bruce Branscomb, address a contestant: "Okay, son, let's see your horse limp." This is said lightly, with a chuckle, but sharp eyes are busy separating the sound horses from the not so sound.

By five o'clock Friday afternoon, all contestants are assembled. Above them the Sierra rise toward Emigrant Pass, which they will ascend before dawn tomorrow.

Heartbreak Number One: Twenty-five riders are eliminated before the race even begins. Those that are passed draw by lot for starting group, then weigh in with their tack—and weights if necessary—to meet the required 165 pounds. Their numbers are scrawled across the rumps of their horses with red grease crayon. They are now ready to take off in the morning.

"We are not infallible," the head veterinarian says over the loudspeaker, "but when we make mistakes, it is always in favor of the horse."

The assembly breaks up—the riders are off to make their last-minute preparations. They have dinner early, and by nine o'clock most have gone to bed. Some of them stay at Olympic Village or at nearby motels, but many sleep in bedrolls beside their horses. The animals stand quietly in their paddocks, or tied to their trailers. Soon all is still as night spreads over the valley.

# thRee

Saturday, 4:45 A.M. It is still dark. The two hundred starters are assembled in the Squaw Valley Arena for the beginning of the ride. There seems to be great confusion and excitement and much milling around, but soon the riders fall into their groups of ten, which will be sent out two minutes apart.

The atmosphere is electric with anticipation. The race has been scheduled for the full of the "Riding Moon," which everyone hopes will be high in the sky tonight, as most of the contestants will finish in the dark, long hours after sunset.

The start in the predawn darkness is eerie, with the timer's voice stridently summoning the ten-horse groups, and the confusion of entrants answering his call. Many horses won't stand still while on the waiting line—some squeal and lash out in frustration. At 5:00 A.M., the first group goes off, and others follow at two-minute intervals, heading west up Emigrant Pass to Squaw Peak and Auburn, one hundred long miles away. They trot rapidly over the rocky trail, which twists and turns its way up the mountainside for almost two thousand feet above the valley. It is cold. Most of the riders wear jackets, which they will shed as the temperature rises.

They cross over Squaw Peak with the wind whipping around them from all directions. The east is beginning to glow. The riders are black silhouettes as they hurry past the Emigrant Trail Monument. Behind them, far below, Lake Tahoe glitters under the rising sun.

I can sense what's going on in their heads: "Rate your horse —ride your own race. Am I moving too fast? Three riders have passed me—is my pace too slow? Should I catch up and let them pace me—or maybe *they* are moving too fast and we'll all run out of gas before we're halfway home."

The riders are beginning to spread out. The trail dips downward into Little American Valley, with much rocky rough going in spots. The careful riders move their horses slowly through this area, because a stone bruise or a twisted fetlock could finish them right there.

In the bright light of morning, I observe all types of riding equipment. There are snaffles and grazing bits, hackamores and half-breeds, Pelhams and "jawbreakers," spades and curbs of all description.

I see stock saddles of all sizes and shapes. Some horses are wearing old Army McClellan saddles with both old and modified rigging and fenders. The flat-saddle riders have varied preferences, with some forward-seat hunting saddles and an occasional deep-seated hack saddle.

One thing the equipment shows, regardless of vintage and style, is hard use! All endurance riders must know and understand their gear if it is to serve them well, for a broken piece of equipment on a night trail can spell disaster.

Riders often dismount and walk or jog alongside their horses to ease the animals. For this reason they need clothing that will be comfortable in or out of the saddle. One young woman wears shorts and sneakers for foot work, with a large sheepskin over the saddle for comfort in riding.

The combinations and modifications of clothing and tack

are for one reason—comfort for both rider and horse that will last for one hundred miles.

The day begins to warm up as the contestants make their way through the Duncan Creek crossing.

The previous evening, after the vet check, Wendell Robie

had cautioned all that, because of the super-dry conditions, anyone caught smoking on the trail would be eliminated from the race. And dry it is, with the dust like powder, ankle deep in places and lifting upward as the horses plod through. Behind the last horse comes the "drag," two security riders who watch for the casualties of the trail. They carry walkie-talkies to call for help when it is needed.

There is shade where the timber stands tall, but in the open the heat is merciless.

At Cougar Rock, about seventeen miles into the trail, the horses clamber up a steep, rocky slope. To the left of them the land falls sharply away into a deep canyon, and beyond it, against the far horizon, I can see Squaw Peak, which the riders crossed about five hours earlier. Some dismount and tail their horses up the jagged incline. Others lead their mounts, but most of them stay in the saddle. Some horses claw their way to the top like cats, digging in, going to their knees. Others do it coolly and calmly, saving their strength for what lies ahead.

The trail gets rocky after they cross the road leading to Robinson Flat, the first check point. The wise rider will walk or jog his horse over this rough ground of Red Star Ridge, for the pace he sets in the rocks could determine whether or not his horse stays sound on this ride.

The scene at Robinson Flat is busy. The "crews" had left Squaw Valley when the race started. Most of them are already here, waiting to give their respective riders a hand when they arrive. The veterinarians and their secretaries are everywhere, doing everything.

At the in gate to Robinson Flat Ranger Station, each rider

A thin-necked horse suffers
less dehydration than a
thick-necked horse.

is handed a slip indicating to which examining station he is to report. The timers have already noted his arrival on their charts. The vets take pulse and respiration. Dehydration is checked by pinching the skin of the neck and noting how quickly it snaps back.

"The thin-necked horse suffers less dehydration than the thick-necked horse—less surface area," explains Dr. Branscomb.

Pressing the gums of the mouth and observing how quickly the salmon-pink color returns is another check for dehydration. The horse is then sponged down and given hay to munch as he dries. After a thirty-minute rest, he is called back for the recovery check. The pulse rate must drop to the mandatory sixty-eight per minute, and of course he must trot out sound.

Heartbreak Number Two. Forty-five horses are eliminated at Robinson Flat.

# four

With the race underway, it's a good time to pause and consider that which inspired it—the Pony Express. Actually it would be difficult to compare the merits of the Pony Express horses with the endurance horses of today, because they performed different jobs. The Tevis Cup horse is asked to go one hundred miles in one day at any gait with one rider. The Pony Express horse was a relay mount that galloped ten to fifteen miles in one day. It was the rider who rode the full one hundred and sometimes more, courting death and danger all the way.

Even though the Pony Express lasted only eighteen months, the glamour and sheer adventure of it expanded with time. And the spirits of the men who rode in it are still able to challenge those who dare to try to match their courage and endurance.

That it fired the nation's imagination is not surprising, for throughout history mail carriers have had great popular ap-

peal. The ancient Greek historian Herodotus produced the unofficial motto of the modern mail service:

> Neither snow, nor rain, nor heat, nor gloom
> of night stops these carriers from the
> swift completion of their appointed rounds.

While everyone with the will to do so can ride in the Tevis no matter how old they are, this did not apply to the Pony Express. An 1860 newspaper advertisement read:

> Wanted: Young, skinny, wiry fellows
> not over 18. Must be expert riders willing
> to face death daily. Orphans preferred.
> Wages $25 per week.

Hundreds applied, but only eighty of the bravest, toughest youths, capable of great bodily endurance, were selected.

There are unsung heroes in every field of endeavor and the Pony Express was no exception. Take Sam Hamilton—the very first rider out of Sacramento. His memorable trip began on a dark, miserable night a few hours after midnight on April 3, 1860. It had been raining for two days and the streets were a sea of mud. On his first three mustang mounts, Sam rode twenty miles through driving rain, mud, and darkness in fifty-nine minutes to Folsom, California. From there the run was even more difficult because the trail to Placerville, California, was a series of steep hills and deep gulleys. The success of the night ride depended largely on the instinct of the ponies. They went down three times in the darkness but the rider managed

to continue into Placerville. Beyond there, the rocky trail wound up in Hangtown Gulch, rising to an elevation of two thousand feet in thirteen miles.

As daylight came, the weather became worse and the rain

changed to sleet. Not very far from a Pony Express station,
Sam's mount went down again. Sam fell heavily, ripping his
cheek against a boulder. He rolled to his knees and blew four
blasts on his horn to alert the relay man. Then he snatched the

mail mochila from his saddle and limped toward the waiting fresh pony. Within three minutes, he was mounted again and galloping up the icy trail toward Sportsman's Hall.

At 6:48 A.M. on April 3, 1860, Sam reached Sportsman's Hall, the end of his run. In four hours and three minutes of rain- and sleet-swept darkness, he had ridden sixty miles over incredibly muddy, treacherous trails, had changed ponies eight times, and climbed four thousand feet into the Sierra Nevada. But he had picked up enough time to give the next rider, Warren Upson, at least a chance of getting over the summit of the Sierra Nevada, despite a raging snowstorm.

"Rough trip, Sam?" Warren asked, as he swung up into the saddle.

"It wasn't half bad," Sam casually replied.

Upson's ride across the icebound Sierra Nevada to Friday's Station near the California-Nevada state line was one of the most difficult in the history of mail carrying; it has become an American classic. The great blizzard had turned the trail into a bleak, frozen no man's land. Blinded by the driving sleet, Upson groped most of the way, at times on foot, leading his floundering pony and clinging desperately to the narrow mountain trails where one careless step meant certain death. But finally he arrived safely at the station with the mail.

These men knew what it meant to endure. Another famous rider was "Pony Bob" Haslam, who made one of the greatest mail rides in American history in March of 1861.

Because of the importance of making fast delivery on President Abraham Lincoln's 1861 Inaugural Address, elaborate preparations had been made to speed the text of the speech from St. Joseph, Missouri, to Sacramento. A fresh pony was stationed every ten miles along the 1966-mile route.

Pony Bob was selected to make the ride over the trail from Smith's Creek, Nevada, to Fort Churchill, an especially hazardous section as the warring Paiutes had been attacking travelers all through that area. Pony Bob received the mochila with President Lincoln's address and sped west, making the fastest run ever to Cold Spring, Nevada, one of the major stops along the trail to Fort Churchill. He had seen no Indians along

the way and figured this was too good to be true. So, at Cold Spring Relay Station, he asked for Old Buck, a horse that could smell an Indian a mile off.

Bob had made a good choice. Between Cold Spring and Fort Churchill he ran into one ambush after another. He eluded them all; then, just when he thought all danger was past, he ran into another as he was coming across a ridge. Old Buck suddenly snorted a warning. An instant later, Indians came from all directions. The rider dropped flat on his horse and

charged right on through. His attackers closed in rapidly. Arrows and bullets screamed past him but miraculously missed their mark.

Ordinarily, Old Buck could have left all the Indians behind, but many of the pursuers were mounted on stolen Pony Express horses, which were much faster than the usual Indian pony. They swept in rapidly for the kill. Given no other choice, Bob drew his pistol and shot the Indians' mounts one by one as they approached until there were only three left.

By this time, Bob was badly wounded. One of the arrows had struck his arm and was buried halfway in with the feathered shaft protruding. He managed to jerk the arrow out, then desperately turned Buck into a narrow canyon, forcing the Indians to fall into single file. With this slight advantage, Bob was able to down two more of his pursuers.

That left one against one. The wounded express rider tossed away his empty revolver and drew his second one. He pulled up Buck and faced his last remaining attacker. The Indian's arrow tore into his cheek, knocking out five teeth and fracturing his jaw. The force of the blow almost lifted Pony Bob out of the saddle. He clung to the saddle horn, and, as the Indian rushed in, Bob's bullet smashed into him at point-blank range.

Bob did not lose consciousness. Old Buck carried him on to the Middle Gate Relay Station. There Bob spent a few minutes caring for his wounds but insisted on finishing his run to Fort Churchill. In this remarkable episode of endurance, the famous Pony Express rider, badly wounded, covered 120 miles in eight hours and ten minutes under circumstances that make most of yesterday's Wild West stories seem tame.

Today, the persons who have risen to the challenge of endurance riding believe, as the Pony Express riders did, in making their horses do what they were intended to do—carry riders over natural terrain for extended periods. True, they are not ambushed by Indians and shot at, but these people are something of a wonder in themselves, since to ride an endurance horse one certainly must endure. The power of enduring means specifically the ability to last, to pursue, to go to the very end—because the enemy, fatigue, is in hot pursuit.

# five

Richard B. Barsaleau, a leading veterinarian, is not only a specialist on endurance horses but is himself a veteran endurance rider. When I was talking to him before the Tevis Cup Ride, I suggested that perhaps his knowledge and experience gave him a decided edge over the other contestants.

Dr. Barsaleau quickly replied that every time he entered a ride he laid his reputation on the line. "How would it look," he asked, "if my horse were eliminated for poor condition? I'd be laughed out of my profession." He had been training and conditioning a five-year-old Thoroughbred mare named Liftaway and he'd entered her in the Tevis that year.

"Now we've all heard it before," he told me. " 'Them Thoroughbreds ain't gonna go no one hundred miles in one day— they ain't made for it!' or, 'You'll be lucky if you get her halfway!' And another, 'Why don't you stick to the Arabian or half-bred? They've treated you darn good in this sport of endurance riding!' "

Well, the doctor was curious as to why there weren't many Thoroughbreds starting and competing. He was convinced that the good Arab or half-bred prospect was the superior endurance horse, but he wanted to see what could be done with a green Thoroughbred—and so he'd bought Liftaway. She was an ordinary-looking bay mare, just about 16 hands and weighing a bit over a thousand pounds. Even though the great racehorse Swaps was her uncle, she evidently was not fast enough to race.

In the beginning she had had a few temperament problems, which might tend to lessen her chances as an endurance horse. She did not load well, she did not tie well, and, worst of all, she could not stand any activity near her without blowing up.

Liftaway was bred to gallop, but she had to be able to trot, because endurance horses don't last long in the rocks at a lope or gallop. So Dr. Barsaleau had worked her at a trot. Trot, trot, and more trot, with plenty of up and down the hills near Folsom Lake, east of Sacramento, till her muscle tone became hard and refined. She also learned to settle down and keep her cool in company.

Liftaway entered her first endurance ride in late April—the fifty-mile American River Ride. Dr. Barsaleau told me about it:

"The beginning of the race was a panic for her—a shotgun start with a real stampede of over 150 horses. Lift thought she

was back at the track and it took me about twenty miles to bring her down to a trot.

"All my schooling seemed to have been for nothing. Her silly plunging and turning and twisting made me think that maybe I should put her back in basic training. But finally she settled down and finished in fair shape.

"At home I continued her schooling," he went on. "Some days I would pony her from another horse, and then I'd drive her from another horse. I would often put Liftaway in regular driving harness, blinkers and all! Many people thought it was a strange way to condition, but I knew the mare was learning trail manners while getting steady increments of work.

"I never put pads on Liftaway's feet. I let her find out for herself that she just could not go clambering over the rocky terrain as if she were running along a sandy beach. She got sole-bruised a couple of times, and before long she began pacing herself whenever she encountered rough going.

"On through June, this mare really started to shape up. By now I was taking her on her first river-crossing trips and getting her to swim in the deep pools of the American River above Auburn.

"Her first attempts at swimming were almost disasterous." Dr. Barsaleau chuckled as he recalled them. "I'd use a long lead line and swim well out in front of her so she didn't have my weight on her shoulders. In the beginning she tried to plunge off the bottom and would nearly somersault. But in a short time she got the hang of it. Once she'd get going I'd drop back and catch her tail and, using that and the lead line, I could pretty much control her.

"She still rushed the hills somewhat but her trot was becoming more cadenced, with less of the goofy scrambling trot of a horse trying to break into a gallop. I find that preparation plus conditioning is the key to endurance riding. Anticipating the problems that lie ahead, and learning to cope with them, is the key to any physical endeavor—and especially endurance riding."

Two weeks before the Tevis Cup, Dr. Barsaleau tapered off the mare's training to bring her up to her best form. The grain ration stayed high but the work was minimal.

By the morning of the hundred-miler, Liftaway was honed

down to a fine, edgy sharpness. She was ready for the big one.

"The first three or four miles off the floor of Squaw Valley is a climb"—the doctor later described that race with obvious relish—"and the ascent is not so gradual, either. We were sweating freely within thirty minutes of the start. Daylight had come, and I could see tiny figures toiling above us as horses that had departed earlier moved on the upper trails. Glancing back, I could see other groups of horses, all making the same run at the hills that we were—at the walk. By then my mare had started to settle into her good hiking stride and I let her march along briskly.

" 'Lots of time for the trot later,' I told her. I sure remembered what these first hills had taken out of my mounts on previous Tevis rides over this terrain.

"At twenty miles out (it was nearly 8:00 A.M.), I stepped off and checked my gear. The saddle had moved back a bit. I walked beside my horse for about half a mile, then remounted.

" 'Now let's see the size of your trot, gal,' I murmured as I legged her out of a walk. She responded nicely and went flying along on the clean stretches, backing down into 'second' on the rough spots and breaking into a jog where it was really rocky and uneven. We kept to this alternate speed up the Red Star Ridge and over Cougar Rock. This famous landmark of the Tevis Ride really makes you get forward to catch a handful of mane and take your weight off your mount's back.

"The going got rough after we crossed to the road leading to Robinson Flat. We tried trotting but finally had to settle for a walk and an occasional stretch of jogging. The day got warm, then hot, and I commenced looking for water. We

64

found some in a stream not more than five miles from Robinson Flat. I let Lift take ten swallows. After a minute I let her have another ten before we moved on. Robinson Flat always had water, so I decided to let her water up there as I cooled her out and groomed her."

Dr. Barsaleau was confident, and had obviously profited from his previous rides. He knew the canyons were most difficult because of the deep descents and steep ascents—not to mention the devastating heat. He strongly believed in taking his weight off his horse's back whenever possible.

"When we checked into Robinson Flat," he continued, "I was pleased to find that Liftaway's pulse was not unduly escalated. I was confident that it would drop below the mandatory 68 per minute after a thirty-minute rest period. I unsaddled and she drank noisily and long. I rubbed her back and gave her some hay to munch. As she dried in the warm sun and soft shadow of the meadow, I felt good and quite relaxed. I downed some salt tablets and sipped some cold fruit juice. On the recovery check Lift's pulse had dropped into the forties and her respirations below eighteen.

"I let her munch more hay—her appetite was enormous as usual, a good sign. I noticed happily that she was well aware of what went on around her without being either overexcited or wearily indifferent.

"It makes all the difference in the world to know just what makes your own individual horse tick—for only then can you recognize any deviations from the norm—and perhaps foresee indications of trouble ahead. But Liftaway was doing great, and soon we were on our way again.

"Thirty-five miles of winding rugged track were behind us, sixty-five more miles of it were still ahead. As we pulled out of Robinson Flat, other riders were coming in. We greeted each other with a wave of the hand or a cheery 'Good luck!' "

# six

Kathy Tellington, riding the Tevis for the first time, told me of her experiences before and during the ride.

"My mount, Windsong, was lent to me by a good friend, Dru Bonner, the secretary director of the ride and the winner of ten buckles.

"I had been itching to ride the Tevis for years, but I never had the horse for it until Dru lent me hers. Windsong was a veteran of the endurance trail, and it certainly was a break for me to ride a horse that 'knew what it was all about.'

"However, Windsong had been turned out to pasture for many months and he would have to be thoroughly conditioned for this grueling event.

"From the first time we met in March, I liked the compact look of this chestnut Arabian gelding with the crooked white blaze running down the middle of his face. I held his head in my hands and gazed into his dark eyes and thought, 'You are still a stranger to me, but time will change that.' He lowered

his head as I gently scratched his forehead—I think I began falling in love with him from that moment.

"At first Windsong was constantly hungry and I kept feeding him as much as he could take. He had also worn his hooves in pasture to the extent that he was far back on his heels, putting undue strain on the tendons.

"The blacksmith did the best he could to correct these foot problems, and after a couple of shoeings Windsong was able to walk out soundly with his weight evenly divided on four feet.

"One of the real tricks with an endurance horse," Kathy continued, "is to teach him to cover ground—moving slowly and in time with his breathing. This will help give him rhythm and coordination. You also try to develop a long trot from the shoulders. My horse only took a month or so to begin feeling strong, so we worked at both distance and precision, using basic training techniques, working on both diagonals and leads. He responded, and in a short time moved with a well-balanced floating action. At times I would tail up hill, just in case it proved necessary on the ride."

Even though Kathy was an experienced horsewoman, she was an inexperienced endurance rider. She wanted to be prepared and anticipate any problem that could occur. She taught Windsong to stand in water and go over bridges. She had the utmost confidence in her horse, but she was taking no chances. She rode him alone and in the company of other horses—sometimes up front and other times trailing along behind.

"In the beginning," Kathy recalled, "when I was conditioning Windsong and myself for the Tevis, I remember being so

cold after riding in the rain all day that I wondered why I even wanted to do the ride. My back felt like a sheet of ice. I was miles from home and alone, but I had to endure. Now I'm not so sure that enduring is the right word—maybe 'learning to enjoy' makes more sense, and this includes being rained on or baked under a blistering sun. At no time past the first couple of months of training do I remember hurting, or being tired. The distances seemed to become shorter. The same scenery became more varied each day. And along the way, Windsong and I became very good friends. I could sense with certainty when he was tired, when he hurt, and when he was enjoying. If there is some magic in the sport, the magic is that of complete communication with a good friend.

"In general I ate, slept, dreamt, talked, walked, thought about the coming ride. It had become the most important thing in my life. I believe that if you don't care too much, it is not difficult to deal with failure—but I cared. It really meant a lot to me, and I was trying as hard as I could. I felt that I *must* not fail. And if I did, it would be all my fault."

At last Kathy and Windsong found themselves in Squaw Valley the Friday before the race—being weighed and checked in by the veterinarians.

"I was totally confident of Windsong," Kathy told me, "until one of the vets discovered a sore spot on my horse's back where the cantle pack had ridden. All I could think of was how stupid I had been to miss a thing like that, and I instantly began to doubt my ability to finish this toughest of all rides."

That night Kathy slept beside her horse, who was tied to her trailer. Her sleep was constantly interrupted by dreams in which she would see herself crossing the finish line again and again. Suddenly she was sliding off the trail into a deep black canyon. She would reach out frantically to save herself, then come awake in a cold sweat. The hours dragged by slowly.

At 3:00 A.M., Kathy crawled out of her sleeping bag. She dressed quickly, and shivered as she zipped up her jacket. A cold wind was blowing down from Emigrant Pass. She fed her horse and hurried over to the Olympic Village Restaurant for some hot coffee and a doughnut.

Back at her trailer she groomed Windsong thoroughly. Her stomach was jumping. Her fingers fumbled with the snaffle bit as she slipped it into place. Next came the saddle pad, then the saddle. When she mounted, Windsong danced in place and tossed his head impatiently. Kathy reached down and tightened her girth as Windsong stepped out, anxious to be on his way. They moved slowly among other mounted contestants —all waiting for their numbers to be called.

Kathy yawned nervously but her stomach felt much better now. The east was beginning to glow.

Ah, there it was at last! Number Five on deck!

"Dawn was about to break when we started," Kathy related. "The first part of the trail is quite steep and it is hard on a horse, because he feels he should keep up with the other horses. Windsong pulled a bit in the beginning, but settled down after we crossed Squaw Peak. Cougar Rock was our next big challenge. My mount climbed it like the pro he was and reached the top with no sweat and moving freely. How-

74

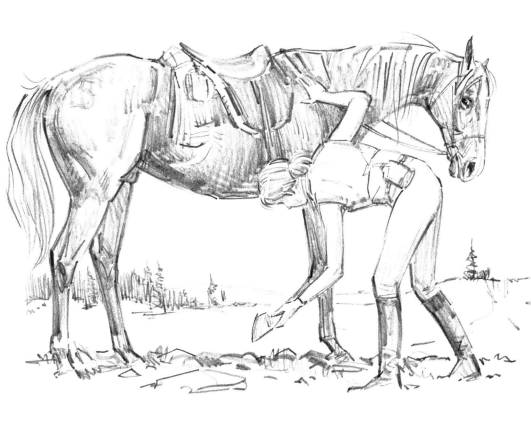

ever, a few miles past Cougar Rock, Windsong took about ten
lame steps. My heart sank—we had come only twenty miles or
more and, if I had trouble now, what could I expect for the
rest of the trip? I pulled off the trail and checked his hooves
for rocks or stone bruises. There were no signs of injury, so I
remounted. The lameness had vanished. I let him walk for the
next few miles, taking it very easy, then asked him to trot out

again—changing to the other diagonal for the next thirty miles.

"I was also worried about the sore spot on Windsong's back that the vet had pointed out. I tried to alleviate any pressure there by standing in the stirrups. To add to my problems, I

was beginning to hurt all over—and this was only the start of the ride! Also, the dust was so thick you couldn't see the trail, which means you must trust your horse's sense of where to put his feet.

"Windsong was a veteran of the Tevis Ride. He had been over this trail several times and probably knew every inch of it. He never stumbled once. My confidence in him and myself increased with the passing miles. I talked to him constantly, reassuring him, telling him how great he was. Seeing that head bobbing ahead of me, watching the changing landscape between those small, alert ears, filled me with a surging joy I had never felt before.

"We arrived at Robinson Flat at 10:30 A.M. My crew was waiting. While I rested, they unsaddled my horse and washed him down, let him eat and drink. His pulse was up when we rode in but, when he was vet-checked half an hour later, it had dropped to a respectable sixty. I was so relieved, and for the first time since we had left Squaw Valley I felt that I might actually finish the ride.

"At eleven-thirty we were off again. It takes a while to build up momentum after a rest stop, so I didn't push it over the rocky terrain of Cavanaugh Ridge. The countryside at this point was breathtaking. Within five miles we hit a dirt road, and just ahead were the canyons where the heat was up to 120 degrees Fahrenheit.

"We moved at a good trot to Last Chance, where we were required to stop for another vet check. Windsong was doing well—within five minutes, by my count, his pulse was sixty-eight. At the start of the ride my anxieties had caused my mus-

cles to tighten and ache. But now, because Windsong's condition was uppermost in my mind, that soreness disappeared.

"We lined up for water, were vet-checked, and took off again. We dropped down into the first canyon, stopped for a good drink in the river below, then headed up to Devil's

Thumb. It was really hot now. I could feel the heat like a fur-
nace blast against my face. We climbed slowly up a steep
winding trail to a fifteen-minute vet check where all the horses
had to recover to a sixty-eight pulse before they were allowed
to go on.

"I was told that many horses had been pulled here, because
the temperature was exceptionally high and the horses had
been moving too fast.

"One of the top horses had run out of gas. The rider was
walking her mount, cooling him out. He would stop and
stretch periodically, trying to urinate, but he was all tied up
behind and too exhausted to relieve himself. I realized then I'd

have to take it much slower from here on in. I was also beginning to understand what endurance was about.

"I had ridden the trail before in sections, but I had never put it all together. I could not move too fast over the rough rocky areas where the path was about as wide as a hoof, with a drop of 150 feet on one side. Nor could we push too fast through the blistering canyons, for obvious reasons. But I could pick up my pace after Michigan Bluff. The only drawback was the fact that most of that stretch would be negotiated at night.

"As the miles rolled by, I kept feeling better and better because I knew now for sure that we would finish.

"We left Michigan Bluff for White Oak Flat about 6:30 P.M. and arrived there just as the sun was beginning to set. The coolness in the air together with a fresh change of clothes and some ice cold juice lifted my spirits to the top. Windsong acted as if he was ready to start fresh and, at 9:30 P.M., we left with the last remnants of daylight on the last 22-mile stretch.

"Starting out of White Oak Flat, I knew it would take me about four to five hours to reach Auburn. This would put me well inside the one-day time limit, so I didn't push. However, we overtook several riders and had good company for about eight miles. For a good deal of the time after dark I had no benefit of the Riding Moon because the trail wound along the dark side of the hills. Luckily I had memorized the trail, but I was constantly amazed at the people who had to do it for the first time in the dark. More than once I picked up riders who asked, 'Do you know where you're going?' Together we would pick our way. By now, company was a help to the horse as well as the rider.

"We were rapidly reaching more familiar territory. Windsong knew he was nearing the end of the ride and picked up his pace. His mind was easy to read, as he trotted up and down the hills he knew so well.

"The trees shone silver and cast strange shadows across the trail. Visibility was very poor, but I trusted Windsong to follow where other horses had gone.

"One more vet check—fifteen minutes and we were off on the last lap of our journey. During the final miles we were alone to No Hands Bridge, beautiful in the moonlight. This bridge is an old railroad tressle, just wide enough to accommodate the tracks, and about one hundred yards long. There are no side rails, and the combined north and middle forks of the American River are 150 feet below.

"It was scary, but it didn't seem to worry Windsong one bit as he moved swiftly across the bridge. In the distance I could see the lights from Robie Drive, the last vet check on top of a steep hill. The climb up the hill was bathed in moonlight; then the trail dipped suddenly into the 'Black Hole of Calcutta,' which is so pitch dark that it makes you feel as though you had been dropped into a black, bottomless pit. This did not shake up Windsong at all, because he knew he was almost home.

"We arrived at Robie Drive at 2:10 A.M. By now Windsong was so starved that he headed for the nearest patch of grass as soon as I dismounted. Then into the saddle once more, and it was less than a mile to the fairgrounds where the ride ends.

"As we approached the stadium, I recalled the first time I had watched someone come in. The rider had cantered to show the crowd how strong his horse was—after all, the whole

idea of the ride is to show that your horse can go one hundred miles in one day and still go on. I was sure no one would be watching me at 2:30 A.M. but, just for the record, I cantered Windsong in and, lo and behold, there were people in the grandstand who cheered as we went by!

84

"At the stabling area I slid to the ground. My knees felt a bit spongy, but the exhilaration inside me was almost unbearable. Dru Bonner and Went Tellington were there to meet us. They untacked Windsong while I sponged his back and head, especially where the bridle had rested. There was no doubt that he was tired, but he stepped out briskly as I led him to the waiting trailer. I stopped at the foot of the ramp and kissed him on the nose.

" 'I love you, Windsong,' I whispered. 'Thank you for being my friend and thank you for a wonderful ride.'

"Then the trailer moved off. It was over!

"The biggest thing I had ever done was over and, if I remember anything, it is how good I felt, and how much fun it had been.

"Suddenly I was completely exhausted. What a long day! Was it only yesterday that I had ridden out of Squaw Valley one hundred miles ago? How sad that a whole year must pass before I would be able to do it again.

"At the Awards Dinner on the night after the Tevis Ride, I was very proud to walk up to the podium and receive my hundred-mile buckle—my first one.

"My back and legs felt stiff as boards and I ached all over. But as my fingers closed on that buckle I knew it had all been worth it, every bit of it. I had achieved what I had been working toward these many months."

At the banquet that night, many other riders received their hundred-mile buckles, including Dr. Barsaleau, who had earned his seventh.

One man, Paige Harper, was awarded his thousand-mile buckle for ten Tevis Rides at that banquet. In his acceptance speech, he summed up the effort and dedication it takes to be a hundred miler.

"Last year I didn't make it within the twenty-four hour limit," he began. "I have a bum ticker and a chronic back problem, and this year my doctor told me it would be plain suicide if I tried again. I told him if I was gonna die, I'd just as soon do it on a horse."

He gave the listening audience a beautiful, triumphant grin and held up his glistening thousand-mile buckle.

"But I made it"—his voice echoed over the loudspeaker—"and I'm here to tell about it!"

# INDEX

89

## ABOUT THE AUTHOR-ARTIST

Sam Savitt and horses have been inseparable practically all of his life. He has written numerous books about horses in all fields, from rodeo to the Maryland Hunt Cup Race. His illustrations have appeared in *Sports Illustrated*, *True*, *Boys' Life*, and other national magazines, as well as in over ninety books. His drawings and paintings of horses have been recognized as some of the finest in the United States.

Pennsylvania-born Sam Savitt and his wife now live on a small farm in North Salem, New York. His favorite pastime—when away from his drawing board—is riding and schooling horses.